Momma, Am I Next?
A COLLABORATIVE PROJECT BY YOUNG LADIES OF ELEGANCE

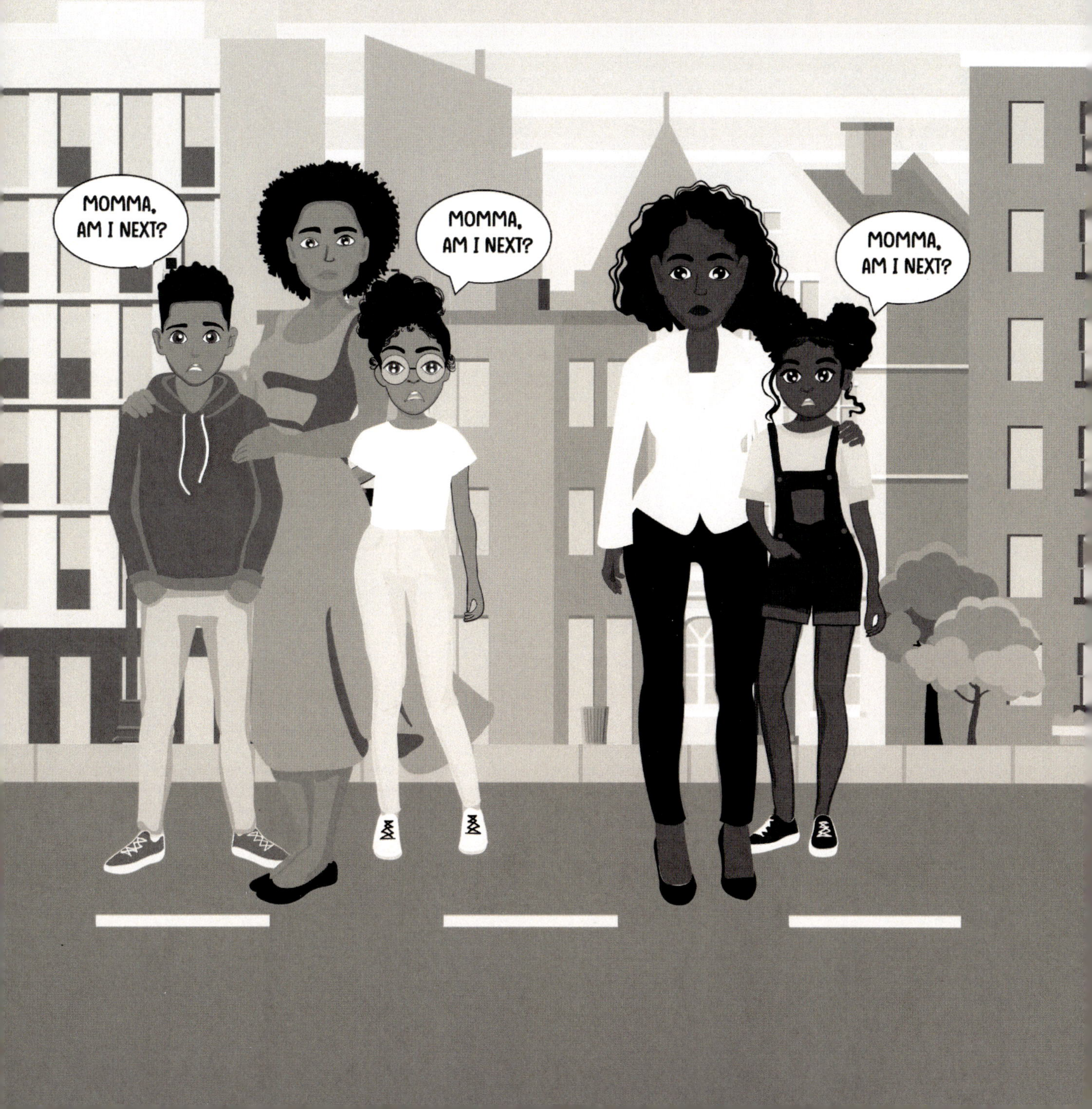

Momma, Am I Next?
A COLLABORATIVE PROJECT BY YOUNG LADIES OF ELEGANCE

Momma, Am I Next?
Written by Y.L.O.E., Dr. Kimberley Booker
© 2025 Y.L.O.E., Dr. Kimberley Booker
All rights reserved.
No part of this publication may be reproduced, distributed, or transmitted in any form or by any means, including photocopying, recording, or other electronic or mechanical methods, without the prior written permission of the publisher, except in the case of brief quotations used in reviews or critical articles.
This is a work of fiction. Names, characters, places, and incidents are either the product of the author's imagination or used fictitiously. Any resemblance to actual persons, living or dead, events, or locales is purely coincidental.
First Edition – 2025
Printed in the United States of America
ISBN: 9798241112347

This book is dedicated to the remarkable members of Young Ladies of Elegance—each young lady who has embraced the journey of growth, confidence, and purpose. You are the heart of this vision and the reason this work exists.

To the parents who have entrusted us with what they hold most dear, thank you for your faith and partnership. To the staff and volunteers who serve tirelessly with passion, integrity, and love—your commitment continues to shape lives and build futures.

To our sponsors, whose generosity and belief in this mission have helped turn vision into reality, your support has made a lasting and meaningful impact.

And to my family—thank you for allowing me to give my time, my heart, my finances, and my love to this organization and to the empowerment of young ladies. Your sacrifice, encouragement, and unwavering support make this work possible.

As the founder, I am deeply grateful for every life touched, every seed planted, and every step taken toward cultivating young women of elegance, excellence, and purpose.

What is this book about? Children worried about being the next victim of police violence or social injustice.

What is the message? The message is to encourage positive critical thinking skills amid adversity.

"Momma, Am I Next?" This question poses a call to action. It is a compilation of poems and scenarios of people living in a world of uncertainty. During these times, some young people are beginning to wonder if they will die at the hand of a policeman, instead of by natural causes.

Questions...

What must one think when they look at television or social media to see a Black person get killed or treated unfairly by the police? What must one think when they see their peers complying with police orders, yet still sadly manage to get beaten or unfortunately murdered at the hands of the police?

One way to tackle the problem is by having honest conversations that include real-life scenarios.

Tyreek's friends overslept, so to avoid being late, he decided to walk to school alone. Tyreek took the route that he and his friends usually take through his neighborhood, which is a gated community. Tyreek is wearing a hoodie that covers his entire head, and he is holding his phone in his right hand.

As Tyreek exits his neighborhood, a police squad car pulls up next to him, and the officer inside asks, "Where are you going?" What should Tyreek do?

Mia and Treyquan decide to go to the 'In & Out' convenience store after school.

Carter, the convenience store security guard, follows them around the store because he thinks they are trying to steal something. Carter asks Treyquan to come to the front of the store because it looks like he stole some candy. Treyquan doesn't have anything in his hands or in his pockets. What should Mia and Treyquan do?

On their way home from school, Julio and Isabella decide to take a shortcut through a vacant lot to avoid getting wet from the rain that is heading their way.

Patricia, the owner of the property, comes running outside and advises them that she called the police because they are trespassing on her property. The police, who were already on patrol nearby, are now pulling up on the property. What should Juilio and Isabella do?

Celie takes her granddaughter Olivia and Olivia's friends, Carly and Emily, to a department store to pick up a few items for an upcoming trip. Celie received an urgent call from a church member, so she stayed in the car to finish her call.

As Olivia and her friends were walking around the store laughing and trying on clothes, Marsha, a shopper in the store, came up to them and said, "You all need to stop playing in this store!" They then witnessed Marsha approach the security guard and point in their direction. What should they do?

Cooper views a graphic scene on his Snap Chat feed of a policeman harassing and beating a complying teenager.

Cooper realizes that the policeman is Officer Nyland, a friend of the family. The incident is broadcast on local and nationwide news.

Some of his friends on the football team said that they are going to participate in the Black Lives Matter Protests. What should Cooper do?

Call to Action:
The police and community must build a better relationship. This can be done by having community forums to discuss problems and develop solutions.

One possible solution is to join a nonprofit organization that provides positive mentorship and leadership programs.

Yound Ladies of Elegance and Young Men of Character are two organizations that readily provide these types of services.

You can also form a community task force that includes local churches, community leaders, and politicians.

EXPRESSIONS THROUGH POETRY

Justice, Love, Peace
By: YLOE Member

Justice, Love, Peace!
We should ALL have EQUAL rights.
Justice, Love, Peace!
We need to stick up for what is right.
Justice, Love, Peace!
Treat people how you want to be treated.
Justice, Love, Peace!
Say NO to racism.
Justice, Love, Peace!
LOVE is all we need.
Justice, Love, Peace!
Because ALL LIVES MATTER!

Walking around America Black. Imagine every day fearing for your life because of the color of your skin. Being scared of the world, but in reality, the world is scared of you. Every day I hear Momma crying and praying for God to keep her baby safe and "protected." Daddy showing me what to do in case of a situation, not understanding what's really going on, but all you can ask is, "Momma, am I next?"

Being scared to speak out and it burns you up inside to stay silent. They won't say their name when you're the one to blame, but they will never feel the pain of being Black. People say they don't see color, but if you don't see color, you don't see me. My Black is powerful, yet you make me feel weak. Just think about it: wanting to make it out of the hood, so you put on a suit and tie, but as soon as "you" put on a hood, you are stereotyped as a gang member.

Or imagine being a single Black mom and you just got a call that your son has been gunned down. "Her baby!" In reality, he did nothing wrong, but the color of his skin was the target. Think about having to bury your child instead of your child burying you. Think about trying to make a "difference," but the difference puts a target on your back. We fought for our rights for over four hundred years.

Who would've thought we'd still be fighting for four hundred more? We were imagining flying cars in the year 2020, not fighting for ours. Everybody wants to say black lives are not the only lives that matter. Yes, that's true, but if one house is burning down, are you going to spray water on the whole neighborhood?

Now think about a nation where everyone is truly equal. It would be nice, but it's time to face reality. We live in a country that is supposed to be the land of the free and the home of the brave. However, everyone is not free. How are we supposed to trust those who serve and protect when we must protect ourselves from the ones that serve?

Who knew that one day a black man would cry out to his mom as he took his last breath? Who knew it was a crime to like Skittles and tea? Who knew that sleeping in the comfort of your own home was a crime? Who knew that jogging while black was a crime? Who knew that being black was a crime?

Slavery is over, but if I scream, "No Justice, No Peace", am I still going to get beat?
Momma said, "You are beautiful" so, my black is beautiful. This beautiful black girl prays every day with a hope that I'm not next. As I talk to mama with my head on her chest I have to ask "MOMMA, AM I NEXT"?
– Kaitlyn Preston

The conversation has begun. Now we must move toward a solution. What's next? Stand up. Speak up. Do something. Your actions could make the DIFFERENCE!

About the Authors

Young Ladies of Elegance (YLOE) was born from a simple but powerful belief: when a girl is taught her worth, she becomes a force the world cannot ignore. Founded by Dr. Kimberley N. Booker, YLOE began as a heartfelt response to the needs she witnessed daily—girls searching for guidance, confidence, and a place where their voices mattered. What started as a small gathering of young ladies eager to learn and grow has blossomed into a transformative movement that continues to shape the lives of girls across the community.

From the very beginning, YLOE was designed to be more than a program—it was created to be a sisterhood. A place where girls could discover the elegance within themselves, not as perfection, but as a posture of excellence, character, and self-respect. Dr. Booker envisioned a space where young ladies would be taught not only how to lead, but how to lead with grace; not only how to dream, but how to pursue those dreams with discipline and purpose.

Through leadership development, etiquette instruction, community service, and intentional mentorship, YLOE guides each participant to explore who she is, what she carries, and who she is becoming. The lessons extend far beyond the moment. Girls learn to speak with confidence, navigate challenges with resilience, advocate for themselves, and serve others with humility. Over the years, parents and teachers have watched quiet girls grow into bold communicators, unsure girls blossom into leaders, and discouraged girls rediscover their brilliance.

What makes Young Ladies of Elegance unique is the heart behind the work. Every workshop, outing, and conversation is designed to affirm the truth that each girl is seen, valued, and capable of greatness. The girls are not shaped into someone else—they are guided to become the best version of themselves.

Today, YLOE stands as a testament to what can happen when intention meets compassion. It is a legacy-building organization committed to preparing

the next generation of young women who will walk into boardrooms, classrooms, stages, and communities with confidence, integrity, and purpose. Because when a girl learns to stand tall in who she is, she not only changes her own life—she changes the world.

About Our Founder

Dr. Kimberley Nicole Booker

My name is Dr. Kimberley Nicole Booker, and my life's work is rooted in one simple belief: when you pour into young people with intention, they rise. I am the Founder and CEO of Young Ladies of Elegance, a program I created because I wanted girls—especially those who may not always see their own brilliance—to understand that they were born with purpose, potential, and power.

My passion for this work didn't begin in a boardroom or a classroom. It began in my own childhood, growing up in Northeast Houston, where I saw firsthand how guidance, encouragement, and high expectations could shape a young person's destiny. As I grew into my role as an educator, I often met girls who were bright and capable, but unsure of who they were or who they could become. I recognized pieces of myself in them, and I also recognized a gap—a need for a space where girls could develop grace, confidence, and a strong sense of self-worth.

Out of that understanding, **Young Ladies of Elegance** was born.

I started the program with a simple vision: to create a safe, nurturing environment where girls could learn to lead with character, embrace their identity, and stand in their excellence. What began as a small effort has now grown into a transformative leadership and empowerment program serving girls across the Houston, Humble, and surrounding areas. I've watched shy girls find their voice, discouraged girls rediscover their purpose, and young women step into leadership roles they once thought were beyond their reach.

Through curated workshops, community service, college readiness events, and intentional mentorship, I guide each young lady to see herself as a leader—capable, intelligent, and worthy. Every lesson, activity, and experience we provide is designed to help them understand that elegance is more than appearance; it is how you carry yourself, how you treat others, and how you choose to show up in the world.

My journey eventually led me to Aldine ISD as a teacher, an Interventionist, a Specialist and now as a Trustee. And even in that role, my heart for young women remains the same. I believe deeply that when we invest in girls, we strengthen families, schools, and entire communities. My work in the district and my work in YLOE are connected by a common purpose: to make sure every child is seen, supported, and equipped to succeed.

Young Ladies of Elegance is more than a program to me—it is my calling. It is the place where I get to witness transformation, celebrate growth, and stand with young women as they discover who they were created to be. Every girl who walks through our doors becomes part of a legacy of excellence, and it is my honor to guide them, uplift them, and watch them lead with grace, confidence, and purpose.